First Look at Languages

My First Look at Italian

by Jenna Lee Gleisner

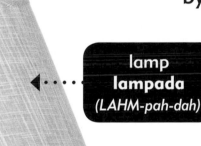

lamp
lampada
(LAHM-pah-dah)

book
libro
(LEE-broh)

Bullfrog
Books

Ideas for Parents and Teachers

Bullfrog Books let children practice reading informational text at the earliest reading levels. Repetition, familiar words, and photo labels support early readers.

Before Reading

- Discuss the cover photo. What does it tell them?
- Read through the introduction on page 4 and book guide on page 5.

Read the Book

- "Walk" through the book and look at the photos. Let the child ask questions. Point out the photo labels. Sound out the words together.
- Read the book to the child, or have him or her read independently.

After Reading

- Prompt the child to think more. Ask: Have you heard or spoken Italian before? Practice saying the Italian words in this book.

Bullfrog Books are published by Jump!
5357 Penn Avenue South
Minneapolis, MN 55419
www.jumplibrary.com

Library of Congress Cataloging-in-Publication Data

Names: Gleisner, Jenna Lee, author.
Title: My first look at Italian / by Jenna Lee Gleisner.
Description: Minneapolis, MN: Jump!, Inc., [2020]
Series: First look at languages | Includes index. |
Audience: Ages: 5–8 | Audience: Grades: K–1
Identifiers: LCCN 2019031281 (print)
LCCN 2019031282 (ebook)
ISBN 9781645273073 (hardcover)
ISBN 9781645273080 (ebook)
Subjects: LCSH: Italian language—Textbooks for foreign speakers—English—Juvenile literature.
Classification: LCC PC1129.E5 G57 2020 (print) |
LCC PC1129.E5 (ebook) | DDC 458.2/421—dc23
LC record available at https://lccn.loc.gov/2019031281
LC ebook record available at https://lccn.loc.gov/2019031282

Editor: Jenna Trnka
Designer: Michelle Sonnek
Translator: Carlotta Dradi

Photo Credits: TheFarAwayKingdom/Shutterstock, cover (top left); Tim UR/Shutterstock, cover (bottom left); ArtCookStudio/Shutterstock, cover (right); Africa Studio/Shutterstock, 1; Quality Master/Shutterstock, 3; Happy Author/Shutterstock, 5; Kyle Lee/Shutterstock, 6, 13; Iurii Stepanov/Shutterstock, 7; KucherAV/Shutterstock, 8–9; kali9/iStock, 10–11; Daisy Daisy/Shutterstock, 12–13; Sergey Novikov/Shutterstock, 14–15; wavebreakmedia/Shutterstock, 16–17; Sergiy Nigeruk/Shutterstock, 18–19; Andrey_Kuzmin/Shutterstock, 20–21 (background); Elenadesign/Shutterstock, 20–21 (foreground); Danny Smythe/Shutterstock, 24.

Printed in the United States of America at Corporate Graphics in North Mankato, Minnesota.

Table of Contents

shirt
maglietta
(mahl-YEHT-tah)

Introduction to Italian

Where Is Italian Spoken?

Italian is spoken in Italy and more than 30 other countries, including Switzerland, Slovenia, and Croatia.

How It Differs from English

- The Italian language uses the same alphabet as English.

- But it does not use the letters J, K, W, X, or Y.

- Unlike the English language, the "h" is silent.

- There are special sounds for "gli" (a "lyee" sound similar to "million") and "gn" (a "ny" sound).

Accents

Accents or marks are sometimes written above vowels. They change the meaning of the letter or word. For example, "e" means "and." But "è" with an accent means "is."

Other times, an accent tells the reader which syllable should be emphasized.

You can speak Italian, too! Let's learn!

Book Guide

This book follows Emma during a typical day. She speaks Italian. We will learn what her family members, teachers, and friends are called in Italian. We will also learn the Italian words for common items we see and use every day.

There are three labels for each word. The first is the English word. The second is the Italian word. The third is how we pronounce, or say, it. The stressed syllable is in uppercase.

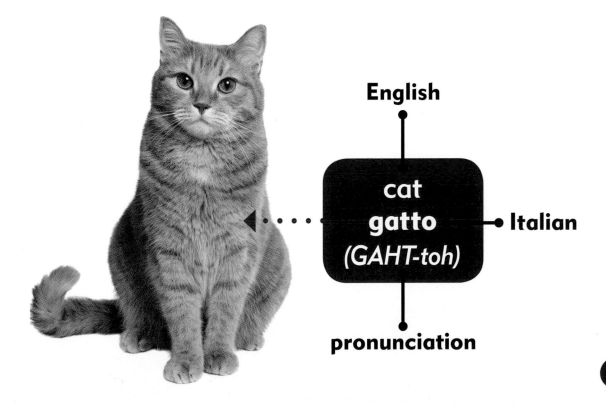

English

cat
gatto
(GAHT-toh)

Italian

pronunciation

Let's Learn Italian!

This is Emma.

Italian

Italiano

(ee-tah-leeAH-noh)

orange
arancia
(ah-RAHN-chah)

strawberry
fragola
(FRAH-goh-lah)

bowl
ciotola
(CHOH-toh-lah)

oatmeal
fiocchi d'avena
(FYOHK-kyh dah-VEH-nah)

Emma eats breakfast.
Oatmeal is her favorite.
Yum!

spoon
cucchiaino
(koohk-kya-HY-noh)

Emma goes to school.
Science class is first.
They look in
a microscope.
Cool!

student
alunno
(ah-LOON-noh)

teacher
insegnante
(in-seh-NYAHN-teh)

science class
classe di scienze
(KLAHS-seh dee SHEHN-tseh)

microscope
microscopio
(mee-kro-SKOH-peeoh)

pencil
matita
(mah-TEE-tah)

paper
carta
(KAHR-tah)

11

music class
lezione di musica
(lets-YOH-neh dee MOOH-zee-kah)

trumpet
tromba
(TROHM-bah)

guitar
chitarra
(kee-TAHR-rah)

clarinet
clarinetto
(klah-ree-NEHT-toh)

drum
tamburo
(tahm-BOO-roh)

12

Music class is next.

Emma plays the flute.

Can you say flute
in Italian?

flute
flauto
(FLOU-toh)

Emma plays basketball after school.

Her friends play, too!

Fun!

basketball court
campo da basket
(KAM-po dah BAHS-keht)

basketball
pallacanestro
(pahl-lah-kah-NEHS-troh)

ball
palla
(PAHL-lah)

friend
amico
(ah-MEE-koh)

basketball hoop
canestro
(kah-NEHS-troh)

15

family
famiglia
(fah-MEEL-yah)

brother
fratello
(frah-TEHL-loh)

father
padre
(PAH-dreh)

mother
madre
(MAH-dreh)

Her family comes.

They cheer for Emma!

sister
sorella
(soh-REHL-lah)

They ride the bus home.
It takes them through the city.

tree
albero
(AHL-beh-roh)

dinner
cena
(CHEH-nah)

salad
insalata
(een-sah-LAH-tah)

chicken
pollo
(POHL-loh)

fork
forchetta
(for-KEHT-tah)

plate
piatto
(PEEAHT-toh)

20

They get home.

They eat dinner together.

It was a good day!

knife
coltello
(kohl-TEHL-loh)

Phrases to Know

Hello!
Ciao!
(chOUh)

Goodbye!
Arrivederci!
(ahr-ree-veh-DEHR-chee)

Yes.
Sì.
(see)

No.
No.
(noh)

Thank you!
Grazie!
(GRAH-tsee-eh)

You're welcome.
Prego.
(PREH-goh)

My name is _____.
Mi chiamo _____.
(mee KYAH-moh)

How are you?
Come va?
(KOH-meh vah)

Colors

red
rosso
(ROHS-soh)

orange
arancione
(ah-rahn-CHOH-neh)

yellow
giallo
(JAHL-loh)

green
verde
(VEHR-deh)

blue
blu
(blooh)

purple
viola
(veeOH-lah)

pink
rosa
(ROH-zah)

brown
marrone
(mahr-ROH-neh)

gray
grigio
(GREE-joh)

black
nero
(NEH-roh)

Numbers

1
uno
(OOH-noh)

2
due
(DOOH-eh)

3
tre
(treh)

4
quattro
(KWAHT-troh)

5
cinque
(CHEEN-kweh)

6
sei
(say)

7
sette
(SEHT-teh)

8
otto
(OHT-toh)

9
nove
(NOH-veh)

10
dieci
(DYEH-chee)

Index

teapot
teiera
(te-YEH-rah)

To Learn More

Finding more information is as easy as 1, 2, 3.

❶ Go to www.factsurfer.com

❷ Enter "myfirstlookatItalian" into the search box.

❸ Click the "Surf" button to see a list of websites.